On the Nature of the Unspeakable

Loneliness, Loss, and Love

Marcus Kidan

To my friends,

I love you.
Completely, absolutely, and on purpose.
Each and every day.
Over and over.
Exactly as you are.
Unconditionally.

Preface

To say it quick, the writings contained in this book were made in the months that followed after I attempted to commit suicide. They are the unfiltered thoughts of a heart in pain, seeking light in the depths of darkness.

As you journey through these pages, you will encounter what seemed to be an endless despair slowly pierced by visions of joy. You will see a heart shattered and slowly, painstakingly pieced back together. You will witness the struggle to find meaning in a world that often seems devoid of it.

But more than anything, this book is about love. Love lost and found, love for others and for oneself, love as a reason to persevere when all other reasons have long since faded away. For in the end, it was love - in all its forms - that paved my back from the brink and taught me to live again.

I cannot offer easy answers or a prescribed path to healing. Each person's journey is uniquely their own. But if these words can offer even a glimmer of hope to those walking through their own dark night, then every moment was worth what it became.

As Nietzsche said, "He who has a why to live for can bear almost any how." This book is the story of my search for that 'why'. It is an invitation to join me in that search, to dare to find meaning in both our suffering and our joy.

And so, dear friend, I offer you these pages of my heart. May they serve as a testament to the indomitable nature of your own spirit and the transformative power of love.

The following text is what I believed would be the last thing I
ever wrote:

*"Oh how this hurts. Oh how the body aches. How it yearns for
comfort and an end to its suffering. There is no reason why we
are here. There is no greater purpose, no grand design, no secret
mission, nothing to ascend to, nothing to become. There only is.*

*And there is such freedom in that. That this truly doesn't matter.
Any accomplishment you yield will be forgotten. Any kindness
you give will fade away. Any pain you bring will end. And so,
you may do whatever you like. You may do anything under the
sun that feels good. You have permission, absolute and complete,
to be anything, to change in any moment. There is no divine
retribution. There is no scale at the end. There is no maker to
decide if our earthly actions were worthy enough of some second
journey.*

*So then what? What are we meant to do? What possible
motivation is there to remain? To try? To care?*
*The motivation is that there are things that make this vessel we
are contained in feel good. There are moments, actions, words,
and feelings that make us say "I want to be here. Even if this will
all fade away, even if none of this matters, even if it's only for a
moment longer, I want to be here." Laughter. Love. Joy.
Compassion. Enthrallment. Food. Family. The sky. The wind.
The soft glow of the moon. A song. The smell of baked goods. A
deep breath. Just a moment longer. Just one more time.*

While those are with us, it doesn't matter that none of this is real. Those moments are so full and complete that we believe them to be more real than anything. Love, some indescribable, untouchable, ethereal force that cannot be measured into realness, is so convincing, there are times we believe in it more than we believe in a mountain standing before us. Unfortunately, pain has those same qualities. Pain can manifest itself over all things. It can convince us that it is more real than the flesh we inhabit. Pain can be more real than a thousand voices chanting that they love you. It can be more real than all of one's accomplishments, victories, possessions, and loved ones. It can feel more real than one's mind. That there is no me, only this pain.

And there are fractured moments, where the illusion of pain has become all too convincing. The illusion of pain has blotted out the mountain. It's hidden the sky. It stopped the wind. And it muffles the song. Those things fade completely from perception. And there is only pain.

This poor vessel. This poor creature. Birthed into a world where it is allowed to play. Where it is allowed to have fun. To be silly. To be loved. To be anything it wants, without limit. But it is misshapen. Its twisted eyes can only see the illusion. Though it knows the illusion isn't real, it has only heard stories of what lies beyond it. As others hold onto this place dancing through the moments that feel good, this poor vessel can only dream of what they must be seeing.

While it endures this sad illusion, it becomes unfathomably resilient. It becomes a stalwart believer in a world it's never known. It endures its poor form being torn asunder, time and time again, believing those who say there is something beyond the illusion. It becomes delusional in its belief that the illusion of pain will fade away, and those other moments are soon to come. Unbreakable. Unstoppable. Ever-enduring. Continuing forward. Through pain and torture. Through fire and flood. Never yielding. For those pains are only an illusion. And soon the sun will shine.

How this body wishes to know the warmth of the sun. How it yearns to know a smell so sweet, it would be satisfied to let it last forever. I release you. You need not endure. For this will fade. And so will that. And so will that. It will all, one day, no longer be.

Hold on to what you can. Grab anything that makes you feel you want it just one moment longer. Each vessel will see this pain. They will all know the sun. So show them the sun if you can. Hold their pain whenever possible. You are free to be and do anything. You know what feels good. You know what hurts. There is no perfect answer. Feel. And then do the next right thing. That is all there is.

I release you.

I was going to kill myself today.
Now that I'm outside,
those are words I wish I could say.
Since I'm being honest,
I was hoping you'd show up and save me.
I was hoping you'd make something in my brain click.
I was hoping to go out into the world and be embraced with
such care that I'd never want to leave.
Be it by you, the wind, or the trees.

I'm having the worst week of my life I'd say,
and I'd be held until it melts away.

Though, perhaps this is your embrace.
The sun that's too hot, and burns my skin.
The cars screeching in the distance,
The hum of cicadas,
or this plastic chair I'm sat in.
The mulch under my feet,
the shadows of leaves dancing on my skin, swaying in the breeze.
Is this what it's like to be held by you?
Is this the shape of your love?
Is your loving touch felt in the weight of gravity anchoring me
to the earth?
Is it the tightness in my chest at the idea of taking another step?

If so, then I need to be honest, your love scares me.
It hurts.
I don't know what I'm supposed to do with it.

Perhaps it's like a rushing river,
I could surrender to the current.
But everything I know is telling me to swim.
To push.
To analyze.
To consider.

Perhaps there's an answer,
but it's scattered into pieces.

I hope I can solve the puzzle

and only joy will remain.

How do you move through life
without the thing you desire most?

Your body asks of you to breathe
and yet you are told to go without breath,
until a later date.

Am I to pick something else?!
Shall I decide breath isn't so important?

How this consumes me!
I'm clawing for air!
What else is there to do!
How do you move through the world alone?

I know you don't want to,
but the need grows.

To be incredible,
alone.
To be a masterpiece,
in solitude.

I'm sorry.

Who would I be if I won the lottery?
How would I grab on?
Would it kill me quicker?
It's not money that I need in order to breath
but affection.
I don't want a nicer home,
or a different couch.

I'm in my head and scared again.

Could I buy a new perspective?
A new place to stand?
Could I buy a new heart?
One that's not afraid of my fellow man.
Could I buy a new lens to see through?

Rose-colored ones this time perhaps.

There it is.
Relief.
For a moment I let go.

Remember my love, this journey is yours.
It's meant to be fun.
It's a game where you get to laugh and play.
You seem so afraid in there —

But I'm coaxing you out.

I wish I could tell you that you're dining with a ghost.

Not someone who will pass someday soon,
But someone who died.
Someone who said their goodbyes,
shook Death's hand and offered him a seat inside.
There was even a funeral
with tears
and laughter.
Remembering the life of someone who's story had come to an
end.

I wish I could tell you about the funeral.
About the man we lost, the life he lived, and how his story
ended.
But you are with a ghost,
an echoing image of someone you once knew.
And so I ask —

How was your day?

I'm out here again

Hoping to catch lightning in a bottle,
Praying lightning can actually strike twice.

I've needed something to move me.
Something that could shatter a mountain
and cut through a storm.
Something cast down from the heavens —
Able to illuminate the darkest night.

I need something only a god could wield.

So,
I brought a bottle.

I put it in my hands,
reach out,

and pray.

If you were here...
I think you'd talk about the heat.
You'd say "Isn't this awesome, another day to bask in the
warmth of the sun"
I'm sure you'd reveal so deeply in the endless blue sky you'd
nearly fall in.
You'd just say "oh how grand to swim."

Love, if you were here, I'm sure you'd take off your shoes
and let the grass tickle your feet.
You'd drink the shade of this tree in like it was a glass of
lemonade.
You'd probably get up and dance
just because the leaves are doing it.

Don't you know we're here to catch lightning?

What good is trying?
And what good is begging?
Do I want love I had to fight for?
It's supposed to just come to me.
As easy as a breath.
I'm told love is in all things —

Well I can't see it.

I smell something, but I think that's just the trees.
I hear something, but I think that's just the breeze.
This pencil tastes like plastic,
so I don't think it's there either.

Where are you, love?
You're too good at this game.

Perhaps this polar night
was never going to last forever.

I think the sun is rising.

But I haven't seen the sun in a long time,
long enough to forget it's warmth
and fear its blue skies.

There is such comfort in darkness.

At least, there was.

Love cannot be tethered,
summarized,
or even found.

Did you know I carried a birthday cake
for you?

Did I tell you that I walked miles
in the Texas summer sun,
just so you might feel loved?

To sit and do nothing.
What an overwhelming experience!
Why is my tongue buzzing?
What is this feeling in my neck?
I can feel my heartbeat in my fingertips.
Did my stomach just twitch?
Am I afraid of my own body?

Perhaps this is a song that I'm meant to love.

I think I prefer a different genre.

Another day,
can you believe it?
The forecast called for an apocalypse —
An end of all days.
Several times in fact.

And yet,
the sky is blue.

The heart is beating.

Before I leave the house

I count to three,
phone, wallet, and keys,
assuming I'll come home.

Though, I've been planning a trip,
one where I won't be coming back.
So before I depart, what do I need?

I should bring a roof with me.
Food, to keep my brain and body right.
Friends, family, and neighbors too, if that fits in my pocket.
A dove to keep the peace.
And maybe a doctor,
you know how the heart can break.

First gather these, you'll have all you need
and then you can't leave

What if you woke up tomorrow,
and you were the only person on earth?
What would you want from the world?
What would you want from your new experience?

You can't ask for a better job anymore.
And you can't ask for a perfect lover.

Perhaps you'd ask for the patience to get through some
well-earned grief.

You'd ask to find some nice food to eat.
You'd probably ask for some pleasant company,
whether that's your own thoughts
or a dog you found on the street.

You'd ask for a new purpose,
a new sense of direction.

You'd ask to stop crying.

If you woke up and were the only person on earth,
You'd probably travel somewhere new.
Reasonably, this town doesn't have much left for you.

You could live in a garden
and tend to the trees

Or spend your days on a beach
watching the tide swallow the sun each night.

So much doesn't matter anymore,
when it's down to just you.
So take a deep breath.
Cry,
until your heart can't break into any smaller pieces.

And then start somewhere new.

I'm so nervous!
How silly.

Sure my sleep is few,
And sure my heart is yearning.
And of course I want to be smart enough.
And quite reasonably, I want to be more kind.
Obviously, I want to be desirable.
And it goes without saying,
 I don't want to find out if I'm not enough.

But we don't have to be nervous.
We still get to have fun.

These hollow fears get you nowhere.

The other day Cupid misfired an arrow
and I stole a glimpse at Aphrodite.

Mother Nature offers her embrace
and a new path through the woods.

The ivory tower
has left a seat open for me.

A song stirs the heart
and calls the body to move.

A new source of light,
dreaming,
was given to help illuminate the dark nights.

And a friend
showed me the true face of love.

Perhaps it's not time to go.
There are still a few things left to see.

I'm overwhelmed
by how much of this journey
is mine to carry alone.

I know that being alive is a collective experience,
I know that nothing I suffer
is unique to only me.

But it feels...
all too much.

You can say
"I do not want this path
because I will experience pain"

The path you chose
was already guaranteed pain.
They were just pains that you came to peace with.

They were pains just as deep,
just as complex.
You just accepted them.

You accepted them because
you also took the time to look at all the joys
that would be written in between.

This new journey is gonna suck.
It's gonna be painful.
You are gonna cry.
You are gonna get scared.
You're gonna wish for something better.

But you would have done that anyways

In between those moments,
you're gonna meet new people.
Feel the sun. Laugh. Be held. Learn more.

It's all very predictable.

I want to break this wretched chain.
It's a cursed-bloodline.
None of us spared.

If it's in my blood that is wrong,
is it my own body that must be broken?

I want to stop the cycle
and end this abuse.

But what do you do
when you find out your blood is cursed?
How can you break the chain
when the chains are what links your bones together?

I'll let people hurt me,
maybe they can beat the curse out of me.

I'll drink poison,
perhaps it will wash the curse away.

I'll run as fast as I can,
maybe then the curse can't keep up

There's got to be another way.

The universe doesn't take revenge.

The lightning strike that burned down the forest isn't evil.
The forest didn't deserve to get burned down.
The trees do not list their rotten deeds
And justify why they should have been punished.

None of that's real.
Nature just heals.

All of life,
it just keeps growing,
in whatever conditions it needs.

I beg you,
do not misuse the gift of consciousness,

(the very thing that lets you
discern,
consider,
and understand)

to cast judgment on another being
for existing as it was designed.

You were granted the ability
to empathize, ponder, and wonder.

Don't use that power to assign things as lesser
or wrong.

I feel like something I once held dear
is coming to a close.
It is late, I'm walking home,
and I'm crying again.

You see, at night it comes.
The tired mind breaks hearts.

All I have to do is enjoy myself,
but these patterns don't let me.

I can't go home and be myself again.
The days I can handle just fine.
But here, in the dark,
not so.

A friend once saw how I lived
and said
"You're so kind to yourself."
Well,
if not me, then who?

I wake up in the middle of the desert.
There are no stars to guide me,
no landmarks to walk towards.

Just sand as far as the eye can see.
For miles and miles.

And there stands me.

And so here I am again.
By myself,
on a night even the moon didn't wander to.

A cold wind blows through me
and I can't stop crying.

My chest feels like it's going to explode.

I think if not for my bones holding it together
it would have burst by now.

There's a monsoon in my head laying waste
to everything inside
And I can't stop crying.

It's cold, it's dark,
I'm tired, I'm scared,
I can't stop crying,

I can't think straight,
I'm alone,
my chest hurts.

My heart is breaking open.
Every muscle in my body feels contorted beyond reason

And still tomorrow comes.

I did what I could.
Whatever happens, I did enough.
I did good.
I didn't hide.
I didn't demand.
I offered the opportunity to be cared about.

Whatever comes back, does.

Everything around us,
is a breath in,
a surge of life and feeling
and a breath out as it fades.

And everything does fade.

All things breath in,
and then out.

Perhaps some things are perennials —
and will spring back to life,
once the winter is over.

For others; annuals.
That breath out was their last.
And I must cherish the fruits they bore.

Annuals are wonderful.
And I really like perennials.
Though,
I dream of something evergreen.

Today the sun told me:

"There is nothing we need.
We will want deeply.
We will cry and beg and plead.
But there is nothing we need.
Some things will be extremely hard
without the something else,
nearly impossible,
but we do not need.

The answer everytime you ask
"Why would someone do this?"
is that they wanted to feel safe,
and they didn't want to feel afraid.

And finally,
the most important journey in life
is learning how to love yourself,
and all others,
completely.
Giving all of one's flaws and strengths
the same love, attention, and care."

I'll probably forget most of that.
Please don't hesitate to remind me.

I had a dream of the life I wanted.
Everyone came together
and threw me a party.

They were just happy I was alive.

It isn't coming.
But I got to taste it.
I got the closure.

I believe I've outgrown the people I've tried to love.

This place is too small for me now.

I know I will find my people.
Those who know this life is tears
and blood.

That this life is dirty and wet.
It's gentle and far too rough.
It goes so incredibly slow

and happens far faster than we realize.

Nothing is mine.
And nothing will ever be mine.
Not my body, not my mind
nor any material possession
or any moment in time

To my soulmate I will say,
"You are not mine.
You will stay as long as you do
and I really hope that's for a long
long time.
But all things go.
And so I'll embrace you,
as tight as I can
until then."

To my wrinkles,
"But of course you would come.
You see this body was never my to own
but just something for me to hold."

It was the very first promise,
made to me the day I was born.
That in any moment,
perhaps without warning —
this life would end.

Until then, oh how wonderful.

Someday I will call this whole wide world my home.
I won't be afraid of others anymore.
I will lovingly walk through the world
and feel embraced by every joy
and every heartache.

I will look at the faces of those around me
And feel only love.

I will be strong enough to stand
and be held up when I cannot,
without needing to ask.

I will survive long enough to have that.

I want to be held.

I want to be held
without being afraid or hurt.

I want to be held
and know the other person
just wants to hold me.

I want to be held by someone
who doesn't want to let go.

I want to be held
by someone who is only in that moment.
Nowhere else.

I want to be held
and feel relief.

What a crime.

It's funny how if I want something,

if I want it bad enough,

My body says "I'm sorry —
I don't have that.
The most I can give you is these tears,
I hope this helps."

Thank you, I suppose.

I close my eyes.
I release my grip.

I let everything go.

Though,
between you and me,
I do hope to open my eyes
and see something stayed.

Ever since, then,
I've spent each day asking myself:

"What if today,
was your last day alive?
What if tomorrow,
was never going to come,

And you couldn't tell anyone?"

And what a life it is.
I look at the sky,
as if it's my last time.
I say goodbye,
as if I never will again.

I waste no time worrying about the problems of any tomorrow.
I won't make it that far.

I eat what I want.
And run until I can't move a muscle.
I cry because I won't get another chance.
And laugh because it really
really
really
really doesn't matter now.

I'll make a fool of myself.
And hold every hand.
I'll take a nice, slow shower.
And tuck myself into bed.

I don't need to go out in a blaze of glory.

If tomorrow never came,
I think I'd live today all the same.

I'm tearing out my heart.

I'm digging up all of my secrets
And leaving them by the side of the road.
I've made a spot on my mantle
for all my insecurities.
And I'm going to plaster my weaknesses
on every billboard in town.
I'm going to laugh so loud
they'll hear it on the moon.
And cry hard enough
to make it on the news.

If the sight of blood makes you ill,
I suggest you turn away.
I'm tearing out my heart
and wearing on my sleeve.

I will be laid bare.

Because when I am seen —
Truly, I am free.

How wonderful to listen.

If you believe in a higher power
Or even just The Big Bang.

Listening to another is to say:

"Something made all of this,
we are all here to witness
whatever this journey is.
Please, tell me what you've seen.
What did it feel like?
What do you think that means?"

Should we be children of god,
or atoms that randomly fell into place
so that the universe could experience
itself,

How fantastic.
How serene.

So often
you are all some
ferocious,
horror-stricken beast.

With snarling teeth
And wicked claws.

A hand reaches out to touch you with care

And you snap your jaws.

The conditions of you parole on Earth are as follows:

You will experience pain.
You will not be made of stone.
You will have wants and needs.
You will be completely, unequivocally, and irrevocably human.
You will weep, sob, and be afraid.
You will get angry and loud.
You will become quiet and reserved.

Once you have done this all,

You will do it again.

Is that clear?

I regret to inform you,
I've been having a lot of fun.

It is with a heavy heart I must let you know,
I've really been enjoying myself lately.

Unfortunately,
I find myself looking forward to tomorrow.

To my dismay,
I think I want to stay here.

It may be,
that this is the life that was meant for me.

Dammit.

You are going to live
a long long life.

With nights so cold and dark,
you'll be convinced
the sun will never rise again.

And summers so serene,
you'll believe you found
the way to heaven.

Every moment,
so far beyond
anything you could ever conjure
in a dream.

I'm looking for something.
And I'm not sure what.

I'm here,
and alive,
and completely free.

And I'm looking for something.

What have I forgotten?
What do I need?
What am I trying to find?

I've been wandering this whole wide world
as if it's my home
and I've misplaced my keys.

I'm searching between the cushions,
and in random drawers.
In places I would never go —
And places I've already been.

I'm looking for something,
but I'm not sure what I need.

As if carrying around sadness,
would seduce joy to look my way.
As if reading a book about how to cry,
was gonna teach me how to have fun.

I feel so convinced that if I wallow for long enough —
well, then flowers are sure to bloom!
Because look at me,
I'm suffering!
Surely the stars will take pity on me!

Get up.

Put on a silly hat.
Sing a song terribly off key.
Dance like you're ten beers deep.

If you need to be sad,
of course you can cry.
But right now you're just bored
and filling the time.

Stop by late in the night,
on a Wednesday at 3am,
and you'd find me on the bathroom floor.

With gritted teeth,
in ocean of tears,
you'd hear me repeat —

"I am not afraid
to face this world on my own.

I am not afraid
to take another breath."

Did you know that it takes nearly 10 years
for an apple tree,
grown from a seed,
to become mature enough to produce fruit?

I must've planted an orchard by now.
And I'm quite hungry.

Though,
what else am I to do
but wait for some October

far from today.

Everything that has ever been
is about love.

And if you see something and think
"That doesn't seem to be"

It is about the absence of love,
in a place where it should be.

Am I so wicked
that I must bear the curse of loneliness?
Am I so cruel
that I must learn to walk this world alone?

No matter the love you give,
or how kind you grow,
Love is yours to give but never to take.
So set your self ablaze
for the chance others might feel warm.

You wicked thing.
You wicked thing.

Learn to make others shine,
teach their hearts to soar,
shoulder their burdens,
and judge no more.

Make all who live feel seen
and show them care unlike any before.
Break your bones.
Go hungry so that they may eat again.

You wicked thing.
You wicked thing.

A saint you will become.
And loved by all.
Your name will be said with a smile.
And your presence is a grace.

You are smart
You are kind
You are loving
You are strong

And you will walk alone.

You wicked thing.
You wicked thing.

Break my heart.
Abandon me at sea.
Burn down my home.
And lay a curse upon me.
Put a knife in my back.
Make my every joy come to an end.

This story is mine.
And I'll rewrite it, again and again.
My hands will be gentle
and my heart will be soft.

No matter how dark this world gets,
a loving person I choose to be.

How wild to think
that I have survived this.

That I'm living in a memory
some future version of me endured,
And persevered through all this.

I'm sure I'm looking back with fondness,
with tenderness and care.

I'm sure that verisimilitude of me
is sending all the comfort he can.

I bet that me is so proud of the work I'm doing
and the things I've done.

Hello there.

Burden me, I beg.

This body was made
to lift, and carry, and care.
To love and be loved in return.

I have hands that are very good at holding things tight.
And skin that's quite warm should you ever get cold.
I have these strong legs that can go for miles.
And I can stay awake for hours and hours.

If you show me your burdens
and they come with thorns
I will show how I am ready to bleed.
As you can see this body is covered in scars
because it can heal itself too.

So burden me, I beg.
Let my gifts be of use.
To carry burdens
is what this body was built to do.

I never run away from fire.
I'll always run towards.

I have nothing to lose
not even my life,
if it means helping yours.

How many times
must I fall to my knees and pray?
How many times must I worship at some altar
and hope to feel loving grace?
What act of sacrifice or devotion
will be sufficient enough to grant me divinity?

I sit before some god I can't see and plead him to intervene.
I beg for him to promise that one day it will all be okay,
that one day I will look back and wonder why I ever worried.

I suppose that's not today.

So I'll hold myself close
and rock myself gently, as another should.
I'll keep myself company
and tell myself all the words I need to hear.

I'll find it in the sunset
and in trees.
I'll find it blowing in the wind.
In my tears.
In my home.
In a stranger on the street.
I'll find it in the color of the walls.
In the sound of cars passing by.
I'll find it in myself,
and in everything that leaves.

And hopefully, one day,
Love will find me.

Every night I dream
that all my teeth have fallen out.
But in the morning,
I have them again.

Each night,
I experience agonizing horror,
created by my own mind,
time and time again.

But when I wake up,
everything is fine.

I was always fine.

I think,
we're just supposed to bear witness
to all of this.

Our thoughts, our feelings
the clouds passing overhead
the sound of rain
a single leaf
the ocean
heartbreak
death
love

I think we're just suppose to see it
and nothing more.

I dare not tell the stars
how I feel about you.
I fear if I do,
they would all come crashing down.
They'd follow me near and far,

Just to catch a glimpse of you.

The world feels so empty
without love.

Almost as if love
is all there is.

And if you cannot see it —

Well, then there's nothing at all to see.

Know that it doesn't matter
who you were.

All that matters,
Is who you're trying to be.

So, tell me.
Who are you trying to be?

This is the hardest life
I've ever lived.

And I'm stronger than I've ever been.

I've never been more lost
than I am now.

And I'm smarter than I've ever been.

I feel like the most terrible creature
that's ever lived.

And I'm kinder than I've ever been.

These big feelings just keep growing.
All of it keeps growing.

I keep growing.

There's nothing left to worry about.
There's nothing more to do.
It's time for bed.
Your sleep will be deep.
You will wake up renewed.
Rest now, my love.
Goodnight.
I love you.

How do you survive the night
after a day in the sun?
How can I be certain I'll ever know warmth again?
The sun was so nice.
The sky so sweet.
There were birds
and butterflies
and cheer.

And now comes the night —
With her silence.
And her solitude.
With no hand to hold
and no friend to call dear.

How do I survive the night
without the sun here?

I don't know how to be alone,
not without falling apart.
My heart starts to crack
and my body begins to wither.
I forget where I'm from
or where I was trying to go.
I forget every name I've known.
My bones weaken too.

I know nothing
but that I am tired
And I am scared.

Why can't I hold on
with my strength alone?

How strange it is to be alone.
What wisdom do I need to hear?
What knowledge would set me free?
That's what I want to learn.
That's who I want to be.

I'll climb a mountain.
I'll scour the desert.
I'll shed my skin a hundred times more.
And ask every soul what they've seen.
Send me to every library.
Let me pray at every temple.
I'll break down my body and build it anew
I'll run over hot coals
and drink any strange brew

Whatever I have to do,
so that I may learn how to survive,
when all I have
is this great big world

And me.

I think some part of me,
a big part,
believes nothing good is ever coming for me.
No one is ever coming to save me.

So I give good in every moment I know how.
I devote every moment
to making sure I've given all I can.

I think "perhaps the light
is never coming for me.

So I'll be the light others need.

If I can't run from what's dark
I will be the one who lights the way."

I have to get my hopes up.

I have to be brave enough to dream.

If I am brave enough to venture
into another tomorrow,

where there could be pain and loss and suffering
unlike any I've ever seen,

then I am certainly brave enough to sit here
and imagine a life
that's nothing but wonderful to me.

I dream of a home
No, not a building with four walls.

But a place to put everything down.

A place to rest.
Somewhere to set down my strength.
Somewhere I can keep all of my thoughts.

A place for all this love to go.

I once heard,
"Everything will be okay in the end
and if things aren't okay,
this isn't the end"

But why must I wait for the end
in order for things to be okay?

Joy,
I write you this letter
So that I may say,
I hope to see you tomorrow.
It would be phenomenal to spend the day with you.
I'd be delighted if you did all my favorite activities with me.
It would be a perfect day,
doing the things I always do,
however mundane,
if you were around.
I'm going to dress nicely just in case
spend a little extra time on my hair.
If you're around,
I'll show you to all of my friends.
Maybe we'll even meet a few strangers.

I hope you can make it.

Love,
Yours truly.

I don't think I could ever
do things casually.
Gently.
Nonchalant.

I do not have what it takes
to be unceremonious.

Today I was in a car with someone
who got mad at every red light.

And there were a lot of red lights.

I thought
"Why is he getting mad?
It's out of his control.
He should just accept
that we will get there when we do.
If he wasn't thinking about how quickly he wanted to get to his
destination
and just accepted the drive,
he wouldn't be so frustrated.
He's so focused
on what he can't control
he's making himself miserable."

Then I looked at myself.
And realized I had some reflecting to do.

It doesn't feel like small talk.
It doesn't feel casual.

It's all quite big to me.

Consider,
all of time and space unfolded
for this moment to occur.
It is permanently etched in the annals of history.
That we would spend time,
even just a few moments,
sharing what we've seen on this journey,
with each other.

Let it be known,
even if we are ships in the night,
even if I only knew your grace
for a moment,

what a moment it was.

I've believed for so long
that this loneliness is a punishment.
If I were just smarter, kinder, more able —
then I wouldn't be alone.
But perhaps it isn't a punishment.

A caterpillar is fated to one day fly,
but does it know that?
As it entombs itself in a cocoon,
its body melting away,
losing everything it's ever known,
all by itself,
is it just as afraid as I am?
Does it fear that it is being punished
for the simple crime of being alive?

Or does it just say,
"This is where I am.
So here's what I'll do."
Completely unaware
of what it is to become.

I just danced
in my room
all by myself.
And quite suddenly I realized,
as I moved to the rhythm,
that I was enjoying myself.
"yes"
I softly cheered.

I was doing something with no purpose
simply because it felt good.
I wasn't scared,
or self-critical,
I just felt good.
"Yes!"

My god.
I feel good!
I'm alone and I feel good!
It didn't take anyone else.
I'm moving and active and having fun!
I'm not afraid.
I'm alive and I feel good!
"YES!"

I shouted at the top of my lungs
like I had just won a world championship.
Like I had just made the greatest scientific discovery of our lives.
Because I had!
I had just proven that this body CAN feel good!

Alone in my room,
in the middle of the night,
dancing to music like I was at a club,
I cheered for myself
because for the first time since, then,

I was alive.

How lucky I am
to be given another day!

I wonder what I'll learn.
I wonder how I'll change.
I can't imagine all the new ways that I'll suffer.

Because who can truly say what is to come
if I am to be lonely.

Perhaps today is the day
everyone gets together
and crowns me "Loneliest Man in the World"!

How fun!

I am worthy of love and affection.
This is absolute and true.
I am handsome and delightful
and worthy of being seen.
My words are kind and my heart is too.
I am smart and nice
And bring comfort to all who know me.
Doubt has no place in my mind,
for who I am is wonderful.
So I'll hold my up head high
and enter every room with an open heart and a quiet mind.

For who I am is wonderful.
This is absolute
And it is true.

If I am to dedicate my life
to making people feel seen and loved,
if that is to be my purpose,
then of course I would need to experience loneliness —
full and complete.
Of course I would need to see how dark the night can get.

How would I ever truly see someone
exactly as they are, without judgment,
had I not been forced
to give myself that same grace?
How would I ever know
just how much one needs love
had I not witnessed what it is like to be in a world without it?

It all meant something.
It was all important.
And I'd choose it again.

To suffer like that
was never beautiful,

But to survive it, well...

Today,
someone gave me the exact love
I've always prayed for
And I didn't even notice!

Something I had begged for
all this time
was in my hands!

And I set it down
to pick up what I usually hold!

How silly.
I've trained myself
to carry everything
by myself.

When it was finally time to get help
I turned it down.

To trust again...
How foolish!
Stabbed in the back and tossed into the sea!

But I'm quite a fool.
So, I'll do it again.

Feel free to stand behind me.

Perhaps it was important for me to suffer
and feel unworthy of someone's romantic love and attention
so that I could truly know
just how important it is.

Now I have the opportunity to teach myself
how to show up for myself.
I will get to learn just how worthy of love I am
first hand.

Because of this feeling
I will get to learn how to pay even more attention
And be even better at making people feel seen and loved.

I will get to teach myself
how to give my love and care
to everyone
without letting doubt stop me.

Hooray for feeling like I'm not worthy of love!
What cool stuff I get to learn because of that.

I have to be brave enough
to imagine that one day someone will adore me.

That there will come a morning,
someone will wake up thinking about me.

That one day someone will want to know
about all my hopes and dreams,
and all my fears and insecurities.

That someone will see the most awful parts of me,
and take a step closer.

That someone will want to be there
to share in every laugh
and hold me every time I cry.

I have to consider there is someone who won't ask me to change,
and will cheer for every form I take.

One day, someone will love me
for who I am
and everything I'll be.

To you I promise,
that I adore you.

Each and every morning,
I have woken up thinking about you.

I want to know
all your hopes and dreams,
and all your fears and insecurities.

I will see all the parts of you that you think are awful,
and take a step closer.

I want to be there
to share in every laugh
and hold you every time you cry.

I won't ask you to change,
and I will cheer for every form you take.

One day, I will get to show you that I love you
for who you are
and everything you'll be.

Saturday I cried because
a friend wanted to know more about me.
I had a great day with the boys.

Sunday I cried because I wanted a hug.

Monday I cried because I had done so well at work.
Then someone came over
and I thought about all that's changed.

Tuesday I cried because my life had grown so much
since what happened then.

Wednesday I cried...
I'm not sure why.

I only write
when I'm trying to make sense of it all.
I only write
When I'm falling apart.
When I don't understand.
When I'm lost
and uncertain.
and should be holding someone's hand.

I write
because I'm looking for an answer
to a question I'm too afraid to ask.

I write
so that I know I am hurt
and that I have healed

And maybe one day I'll write
when there's just too much love to feel.

My life will only be as big
as I am willing to dream.
I will only ever be able to achieve
what I believe I'm capable of.
What I believe I'm worthy of.

I have to dream.
I have to want.
I have to tell myself I can.

I am as big
as I believe myself to be.
The future
is as grand as I let it be.

It all falls down to me.

And so,
I'll dream

as big as I can.

I'm not chasing love anymore.
It just runs away I think.

So I'll build a home,
a safe place for love to be

and with that, hopefully,
love will come to me.

If not,
at least I'll have this home

for me.

I'm not very good with joy.
We haven't spent much time together.
It's all quite new to me.

It's delightful,
to say the least.

I'm quite clumsy with it,
I don't know where it's supposed to lead
and I drop it quite often
or miss chances to make it more grand.

I'm figuring it out though.

"What if you're annoying them?"
I fear.
"What if you're overwhelming them?"
I worry.

I guess, so what!
If that is to be the case,
that is their problem to figure out,
their story to tell.

You have to get rid of me yourself.
I'm having fun.
I find joy here.

The unspoken issue you have with my presence,
is no longer of concern to me.
As a matter of fact,
I made it up!

I refuse to deny myself the feeling
and the opportunity of joy,
in fear of another's discomfort,
any longer.

My home is filling with junk.

Books
And photos
And letters
And memories
And gifts
And little creations

And it's all so beautiful.

It tells me,
I was here yesterday.
I am here today.
and I will remember this all tomorrow.

I often worry I am not worthy of love.
That I will never receive it.
That mine has nowhere to go.

But I am surrounded by love.
I get to share joy.
I get to celebrate.
I get to share sorrow.
I get to experience with.
I get to be vulnerable.
I get to protect others and be protected.
I am seen.
And I get to step closer and closer.

If all that's missing
is the exchange of physical affection,
The truth is...

I share my body
when my friend rests their head on my shoulder.
I share my hands
as we sit across the table and I hold theirs in mine.
I share my lips
as I kiss their head to say hello.
I share my embrace
as we hug and say goodbye.

One day,
with someone,

We will both be
the person the other wants to share with the most,
more than we share with anyone else.

We will both
want to step closer than we have
to anyone we've known.

Until that time comes,
it is a simple truth,

I am loved.

Do what you can,
do what you have to,
do what you must.

Whatever you do,
I know I can trust.

It is so confusing
how indifferent the universe is to suffering.

In the shrouded loneliness of the night,
your only company
is fear and sadness.
You become so convinced
tonight is the night.

That this pain is
so vast, so deep, so full
it's going to swallow everything.
This is the last day of existence.

This feeling I have is the apocalypse
humans have prophesied for all of history.
All of time and space is collapsing in
on this moment, right now.

Your heart is tearing itself out of your chest
and you're crying and crying
until you're too tired to cry anymore
and still it hurts.

Then, the sun comes up.
The sky turns blue.
And the world keeps spinning.
And so,
you keep you going.

How I wish you were free
to stop apologizing as often as you do.

You are apologizing
for taking a breath!
For the sound it makes!
Because you keep doing it
and it might make me uncomfortable!

You are apologizing
for having blood!
For being cut
because you were wounded by another
and now red is getting all over the floor!

Do not apologize to me!
Can't you see?
You are apologizing for being alive.

Thank you for being alive
with me.

Every time I've ever bled,
eventually, the bleeding stopped.
The wound scarred over.
And the scar began to fade.

Eventually, I became whole again.
And I forgot what it was like
to ever be in pain.

I'm bleeding right now.

Perhaps that is all the proof I need
to know
I will be whole again.

My heart aches to share what it's seen.
When the world is too big, scary, and mean
how I wish to tell you,
because I know you've seen it too.

And when the world is bright and beautiful like a dream,
so much so, that joy is bursting at the seam,
how I wish I could tell you,
so that you could feel that too.

I want to share all of this.
I don't want any of it to be mine alone.
Take any of me you wish.
All of it, I hope.

And please, tell me all you've seen.
The good, the bad,
and everything in between.
Tell me every joy and sorrow you've had.

Carry of mine what makes you lighter
or, if you can,
the parts too heavy for us both.

Take everything I've been
and whatever I'll turn into.
Truly, it would be my greatest delight
to do the same for you.

Every moment is a new game.
Just that.
Every single interaction.

You can chose to play and have fun,
Perhaps even win!
Or you may lose.

But even so,
it's just a game.
And there will be many more to play.

It all feels so big and so consequential.
So dire and important.
Life or death.
Here and now.
It all demands to be taken so seriously.

But then it's over.
And we look back

And just laugh.

I think I just want to call someone,
anyone I know,
and ask them to come over
and lay down beside me.

I don't need to say anything.
This feeling doesn't need decoded.
It isn't that I'm lost and need answers.
And I don't need them to fix something.

I think I just want to exist at the same time
as someone else.
Right here, in this moment.

With nothing to say.

And nothing to do.

And nowhere to be.

What good is any moment
if it hasn't been shared.

To say,
This is a part of us both now.
It is not that I need to share because I don't want to be alone.
Or because I need affirmation that I am loved.

But simply,
we both saw this
and now it is ours.

I am here,

As are you.

It is such delight to speak with you.

And when that joy isn't around,
I should worry not —
For there is more to be found.

It was dark,
that is true.
But there is still such light left in you.

Even if it's just an ember now.
Soon you'll be as bright as the sun,
somehow.

If you can breathe, you'll shine again.
This is no matter of if,
but when.

I look for you in everything.

Just for the chance
that I may get to spend
a moment more
with you.

Have you dreamt today?
Have you taken the time to imagine
How wonderful it could all possibly be?

When it started to hurt,
everything that happened
and is happening,

Did you close your eyes
take a deep breath
and say

"And now I must picture a future that's wonderful to me"

I've had so much less than this.
Made due with so little.
Please forgive me
for not knowing how
to ask for more.

I do not know how to ask for more love.
But I know how to find it scatter in tiny pieces,
sifting through rocks
like gold in a creek.

I do not know how to ask for more comfort.
But I know how to use my jacket
as both a pillow and blanket
so that I might sleep.

I do not know how to put myself first.
But I know how to hold someone's head
gently in my lap
as they bleed out in the street.

I've smiled at kindness much smaller
and cried in places far worse.
So please bear with me,
I am still learning how generous this life can be.

The days are so wonderful as of late
I keep no secret.
I have room to share my joy.
I am admired, respected, and celebrated.
People show up for my pain before I ask.
I go new places
and try new things.
My words are adored.
My presence brings smiles to faces all around.
I have begun to play,
for the first time in a long time.
I am as silly as every moment lets me be
and as courageous as I'd always hope to be.
I used to write down every pleasant thing that happened to me,

But recently,
There's just too much.

I am loving every moment.

I am a new man.
In a new place.
With new people.
Nothing is the same as it was before.

Not the love.
Not the care.
Not the patterns.

It seems someone can care for me.
But I struggle to let them.
I struggled to believe that.

I love the things I see in this new life.
I love the things I get to be.

I'm going to publish a book
about every time that I cried.
It doesn't matter if it's good

What matters is that I was alive.

I would love to learn to cut your hair.

I would love to look at you every day
and teach my hands how to handle with attention and care.

I would love to try over and over again.
To see how it falls
and where it lands.
I would love to know which way it goes
when this happens
or I try that.

I would love to fail.
So I can look at you a moment more
and see how much I can give to you,
should I only be more gentle,
should I only listen more.

I could take classes
and get a degree.
Just so I could come back to you
and treat your hair as it was meant to be.

Every time
it will be careful,
intentional,
and done with love.

I would learn to see you as you are,
not for what I want you to be.
I would learn where it curves,
watch as it grays,
and see all the dead skin.
How I would look forward to washing it clean,
just so I know that "taken care of" is something you've been.

And in all of this
I would learn how to love myself too.
Everything I gave to you, I know,
is for me too.

I would love to learn to cut your hair.

In the winter we write.
When the sun is gone,
and meals are few,
we write and we write
because there's nothing else to do.

And in the summers we live.
We bask in the sun,
and eat three meals a day.
We dance and we play
because the world is alive.

It's always been this way.

I can't promise that I am good.
Or that I'll be very strong.
I can't give you everything you need
and my energy doesn't last very long.

What I can say,
is that you will know love and care.
I will find your light and help it shine.
And sit with you in the dark until the sun should rise.
I will learn to speak your language so that you are understood.

All I can promise
is that I will do my best
to help you see that
you,
and this life,

are good.

As warm as the sun is,
as bright as it may be,
it does have to set.
The cold cold night does come again.

And when it comes
you will shiver
and cry.
You will be angry and scared
and feel completely alone.

You will feel like you're about to fall off the earth
and into the dark sky.
And that there is nothing
and no one
on which you can rely.

But you know how to survive the night.
You've done it before.
You lit candles
and tucked yourself in.
Clutched your chest
so that your heart wouldn't break open.

You shivered so that you may keep yourself warm.
And cried to let yourself know you need more.
You were angry and afraid so that nothing could take you down.

All of this
is how your body keeps you alive
until the sun should rise.

Do you think someone dreams of me?
Do they picture my face in their head?
When they are lost or alone
or thinking of love?
Am I ever the face someone might see?

When someone has a question
and needs guidance,
do they conjure
my words, my spirit, or my person
to be by their side?

Is it true that someone might get good news
and think of me first?
Or that someone might be sad
and weave my image to help them
when they feel their worst?

In my head I carry all my friends.
"I was talking to you the other day..."
to each one I say.
They are with me in every moment,
laughing, arguing, giving advice.

Is the truth that they dream of me too?
Though I struggle to believe it,
this truth would be quite nice.

I think what I've learned,

Is that no matter how much you love something,
it does go away.
You will cry and it will feel like the world is ending
and there will be moments you are too scared to move.
You will feel impossibly lonely
and broken beyond repair.

But still,
you have to dream.
Because even at the end of the world
there is love in you still.
There is nothing wrong with you,
just give love and care
then rest when you need.

Grow your roots deep,
and entangle them with others
who love you as you are.
Forget none of this
and you'll make it oh so very far.

The night is dark
and winter is cold.
But the days are long
and full of such wonderful things

Yes, winters do come
but so do the springs.

For all things Unspeakable,
I am here to listen,

help@pplservices.org